THE ULTIMATE BEGINNER SERIES

ROCK BASS BA

STEPS ONE & TWO COMBINED

TIM BOGART   ALBERT NIGRO

Editor: Aaron Stang
Cover Layout: Joann Carrera
Technical Editor: Glyn Dryhurst
Engraver: Charylu Roberts

Introduction

Welcome to the world of rock bass. *The Ultimate Beginner Series - Rock Bass* will help to get you started as a rock bass player. This book will show you some classic rock grooves and bass lines that every rock bass player needs to know, various right and left hand techniques, quarter, eighth and sixteenth note feels, how to work rhythmically with a drummer, and some special techniques, such as harmonics, tapping and double-stops. All of the classic bass lines have also been recorded for you to hear and play along with.

CONTENTS

HOW TO TUNE UP

Electric Tuners:

Many brands of small, battery operated tuners, similar to the one shown below, are available. Simply follow the instructions supplied with your tuner.

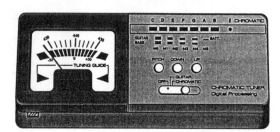

Tuning to a Piano or Electronic Keyboard:

An easy way to tune a bass is to a piano keyboard. The four strings of the bass are tuned to the keyboard notes shown in the following diagram.

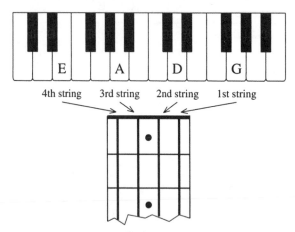

Tuning the Bass to Itself (Relative Tuning):

1. Tune the 1st string to G on the piano (or some other fixed pitch instrument, such as a pitch pipe).

2. Depress the 2nd string at the 5th fret. Play it and you will hear the note G, the same as the 1st string open. Turn the 2nd string tuning key until the pitch of the 2nd string matches of that of the 1st string.

3. Depress the 3rd string at the 5th fret. Play it and you will hear the note D, the same as the 2nd string open. Turn the 3rd string tuning key until the pitch of the 3rd string matches that of the 2nd string.

4. Depress the 4th string at the 5th fret. Play it and you will hear the note A, the same as the 3rd string open. Turn the 4th string tuning key until the pitch of the 4th string matches that of the 3rd string.

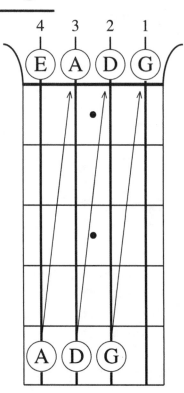

MUSIC NOTATION

The rhythms and note names are indicated by the standard notation, and the location of those notes on the neck of the bass is indicated by the tablature. Here are some basic rules of standard notation:

Music is written on a staff, which consists of five lines and four spaces (between the lines):

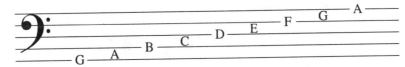

At the beginning of the staff is a bass clef (or F clef). The bass clef is used for all bass instruments.

The notes are written on the staff in alphabetical order. The first line is G:

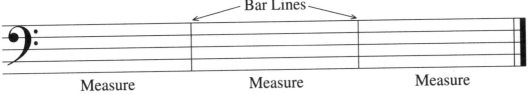

The staff is divided into *measures* by *bar lines.* A heavy double bar line marks the end of the music:

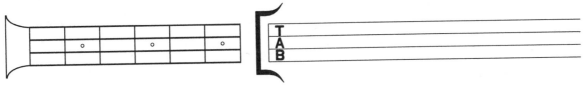

Tablature

Tablature is commonly used in conjunction with standard music notation. Tablature illustrates the location of notes on the neck of the bass. This illustration compares the four strings of a bass to the four lines of tablature.

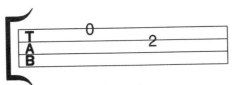

Notes are indicated by placing fret numbers on the strings. An "O" indicates an open string.

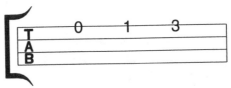

This tablature indicates to play the open, 1st, and 3rd frets on the 1st string.

RHYTHM NOTATION AND TIME SIGNATURES

At the beginning of every song is a time signature. 4/4 is the most common time signature:

4 Four counts to a measure
4 A Quarter note receives one count

The top number tells how many counts per measure, the bottom number tells which kind of note receives one count.

The time value is determined by three things:

1) note head: o   •

2) stem:

3) flag:

o   This is a whole note. The note head is open and has no stem.
    In 4/4 time, a whole note receives 4 counts.

    This is a half note. It has an open note head and a stem.
    A half note receives 2 counts.

    This is a quarter note. It has a solid note head and a stem.
    A quarter note receives 1 count.

    This is an eighth note. It has a solid note head and a stem with a flag attached.
    An eighth note receives 1/2 count.

Whole Note: o			
Count: *1*	*2*	*3*	*4*
Half Note:			
Count: *1*	*2*	*3*	*4*
Quarter Note:			
Count: *1*	*2*	*3*	*4*
Eighth Note:			
Count: *1* & *2* & *3* & *4* &			

RIGHT HAND TECHNIQUES

CD
(3) When playing the examples, there are several different tone qualities that you can create with your right hand without ever touching the tone control knob on your bass or amplifier. This is done by positioning the right hand at various places on the bass and is necessary to achieve the correct sound for the style you are playing.

When playing ballads and long notes, such as whole and half notes, play up near the neck; this gives a full, rich sound.

When playing quarter and eighth note feels, play directly over the pickups; this gives a more percussive sound.

When playing sixteenth note feels, play back by the bridge; this gives a thinner, tighter sound with more definition.

ROCK BALLAD FEELS

Throughout this book we will cover many different classic rock grooves; some of them are fast sixteenth note rock feels, others are slow ballads and some even use power chords. Each one will help develop the techniques that you will need to know as a rock bass player. One of the most important things you need to be able to do as a rock bass player is to lock in with the drummer. This is done by matching the subdivision (the way each beat is subdivided) the drummer is projecting. Listen to the included recording to hear how to do this. Play along to help practice locking in. The first groove we will cover is a slow rock ballad.

CD ④ *Example 1: Slow Ballad*

This example demonstrates a slow ballad feel in the key of G major. A ballad is usually characterized as having a slow tempo and sad or melancholy quality. The example alternates between the root of the I chord (G) and the vi chord (Em), using a dotted quarter to eighth note feel. There is also a connecting line leading from the root of each chord, moving down chromatically from the G to the E and back up chromatically from the E to the G. This gives the line a little character in addition to connecting the roots of the chords. A chromatic connecting line moves up or down by half steps, sounding every pitch between the roots. Use your left hand to achieve separation between the notes by releasing the pressure on the string, lifting the string off of the fretboard to stop it from ringing.

CD
(5) # *Example 2: "Stand By Me" Ballad*

This example is another ballad feel. This one is similar to the song "Stand By Me" by Ben E. King. It is in the key of C major and moves in a standard I (C), vi (Am), IV (F), V (G) chord progression. To help make a smooth transition between the roots of the chords, this example uses **diatonic** rather than chromatic connecting lines (meaning the notes are from a particular scale, in this case C major).

CD (6) # *Scales*

Before moving on to the next example, there are two scales that you are going to need to know. As a rock bassist, you are going to find you do not need to know that many scales, but these two are very important. They are the major and minor pentatonic scales, and they contain the five primary notes from the major and minor scales.

First is the **major pentatonic**, which uses the root, second, third, fifth and sixth of the major scale.

E Major Scale:	E	F♯	G♯	A	B	C♯	D♯	E
	1	2	3	4	5	6	7	8
E Major Pentatonic:	E	F♯	G♯		B	C♯		E

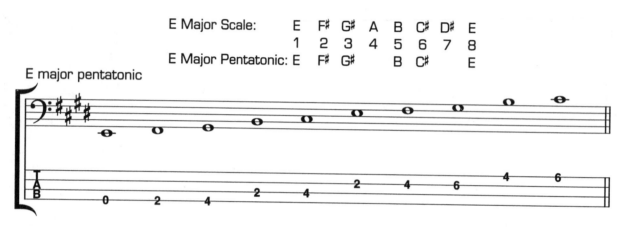

Next is the **minor pentatonic**, which uses the root, third, fourth, fifth and seventh of the minor scale.

E Minor Scale:	E	F♯	G	A	B	C	D	E
	1	2	3	4	5	6	7	8
E Minor Pentatonic:	E		G	A	B		D	E

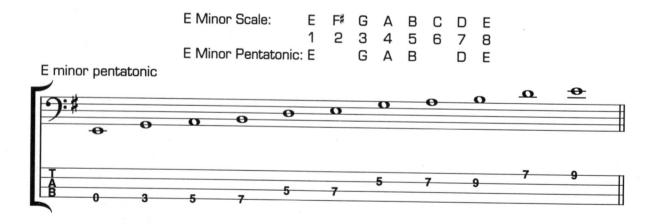

Both scales are demonstrated here using E as the root, but can be transposed to use any note as the root.

CD ⑦ *Example 3: "My Girl" Riff*

This example uses the E and A major pentatonic scales, starting on the root and ascending to the octave. It is based on the immortal bass line of the popular tune "My Girl" by the Temptations. It also contains a common line that walks down from the V chord (B7) to the I (E) which brings you back to the top of the song. This is sometimes called the **turnaround**.

This example transposes the "My Girl" riff to E minor, giving it a darker, heavier sound.

Minor pentatonic "My Girl" riff:

CD 8 Example 4: Ballad with Passing Tones

This is another example of a ballad that uses passing tones. It starts on the I chord (E), walks down the major scale to the vi chord (C♯m) with the D♯ as a passing tone, then down to the IV chord (A) with the B as a passing tone, then down to the ii chord (F♯m) with the G♯ as a passing tone, then walks up the E major scale, using the A♯ and D♮ as chromatic passing tones. This chord progression is very common and can be found in many popular rock and country ballads.

Example 5

This example is a ballad feel in the key of C, introducing what is known as the **slash chord** (G/B). A slash chord occurs when the bass note is not the root of the chord, but is instead another chord tone, such as the third or fifth. This example uses several slash chords such as the G/B chord, where the bass is playing B (the third of the G chord), not the root. The example primarily descends through the C major scale and uses mostly half notes. Be sure to make the "right hand feel" consistent and all the notes the same length. Listen to, and lock in with, the drummer.

QUARTER NOTE ROCK FEELS

This next section covers several quarter note rock feels. The feel of quarter note roots and simple lines is common to what is known as "stadium rock." When playing large venues, the bass player, when he or she gets too busy, will not be heard in the hall. Most of the exercises in this section concentrate on this quarter note feel.

CD
(10) *Example 6*

This example uses quarter note roots throughout, alternating between A and G. To keep the example interesting there are several eighth note lines connecting each chord change, leading up chromatically or down diatonically to the root of the next chord.

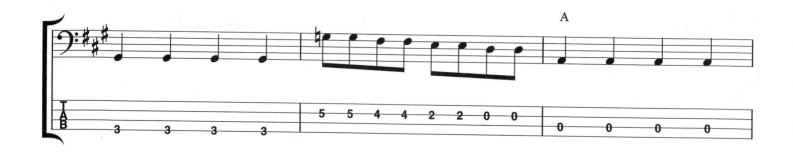

CD
(11) ## *Example 7: Slide and Hammer-on*

This next example uses two new techniques: the **slide** and the **hammer-on**. To slide from one pitch to another, simply play a note and slide your finger to the next note, keeping pressure on the string. The hammer-on is done by hammering the string to the fretboard using the tip of any left hand finger. The note is sounded by the left hand attack (the right hand is not used).

CD 12

Example 8: "Rolling Stones Feel"

This example is very similar to many of the lines used by Rolling Stones bassist Bill Wyman. It uses the root, fifth and sixth of the chord, moving down then up the pattern. The pattern is based on the major pentatonic scale, using three of the five notes of the scale.

Example 9

This is very similar to Example 8, except it is based on the minor, rather than the major, pentatonic scale. The pattern is played over a 12-bar minor blues—a common song form.

CD 14 Example 10: Ostinato Bass

This example introduces a technique known as **ostinato bass**. Ostinato is a big word which basically means that while the chords move, the bass note doesn't. In this case the bass pedals an E underneath the chords, starting on the low E and then adding the octave above as the dynamic level of the song rises, to make the feel more intense. Remember to be consistent with the "right hand feel" so that each note sounds similar to the next.

CD (15) *Example 11*

Here we use the major pentatonic scale in what is known as an "and" feel. This is also referred to as syncopation, where the notes are played primarily on the up-beats. The up-beats are in-between the beats, and are called "and" (1 and 2 and 3 and 4 and). This example plays on beat 1, and then on the "ands" of beats 2, 3 and 4.

Beats: 1 (and 2) and (3) and (4) and

Practice counting the rhythm aloud and listen to the recorded example to get the feel of the rhythm.

EIGHTH NOTE ROCK FEELS

This next section covers several eighth-note rock grooves. The exercises are similar to the exercises in the previous section in that they are mostly roots and simple passing lines, but using primarily eighth notes instead of quarter notes (two notes per beat instead of one). Be sure to alternate your left hand fingers when you practice to help increase your speed.

CD ⑯ *Example 12: "ZZ Top Groove"*

This example uses a groove similar to a song by the legendary rock band ZZ Top. This one is mostly roots with a chromatic line approaching each chord change, giving the impression of a "walking" movement. The example also adds the II chord (Am) and ends with some upper register **double-stops** and **chords.** Double-stops refer to playing more than one note at a time and are usually done in the upper register of the bass due to the overall low range of the instrument. When lower range notes are played together, they tend to sound muddy and the pitches are hard to perceive.

CD (17) *Example 13*

This example is the same as Example 12, except it is indicated to play the notes **staccato** (by the dots over and under the note heads). Staccato means that the note is cut off sharply by stopping the string from vibrating. This can be done by releasing the pressure in the left hand, lifting the finger slightly off of the fretboard but not off of the string. Playing staccato makes the feel much sharper.

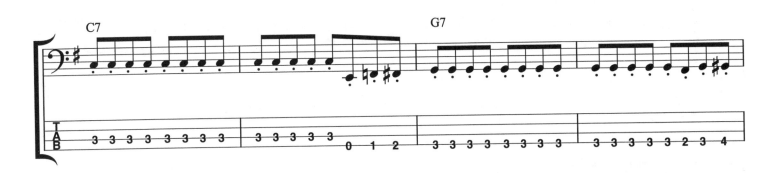

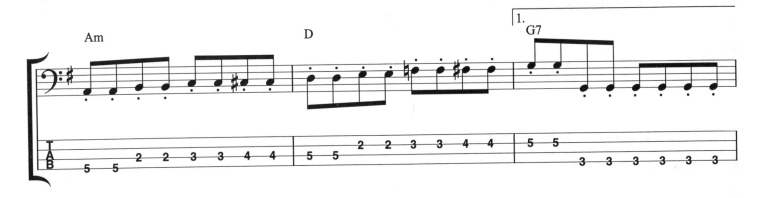

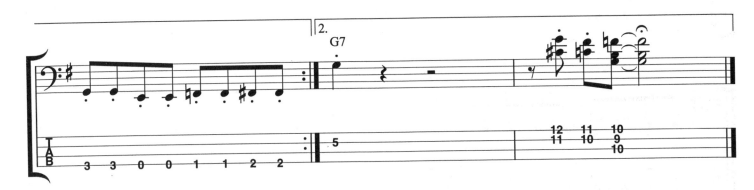

Example 14

Here is an eighth note pattern in the key of E, using the root, fifth and flat seventh of the scale. To help solidify the groove there is a sixteenth note lick at the end of each phrase emulating a pattern played by the drums. The notes in this lick are muted. It is easier to play if the index finger is dragged across the strings, a technique commonly known as "raking."

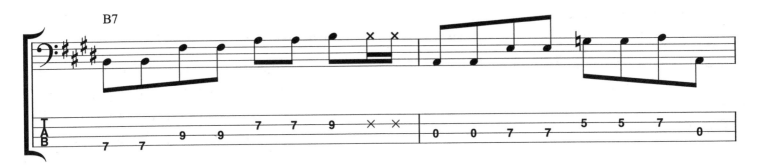

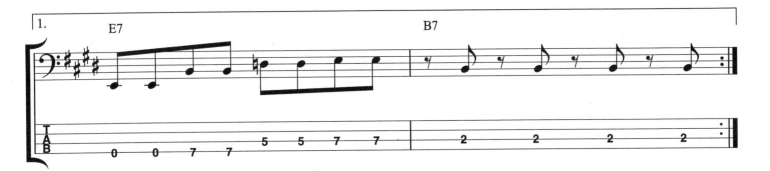

Example 15

This next eighth-note example can be divided into two sections. The first section uses ostinato bass (where the chords move but the bass note doesn't). In the second section, the bass line follows the chord changes, which makes the tune sound different. Remember to practice alternating the right hand fingers, keeping the notes steady and hitting the strings with the same finger pressure; that way the volume will be consistent.

Example 16

This one uses most of the notes in the major pentatonic scale plus the flat third. The technique of using both the minor and major third is very common to rock and blues. The example uses both **open** and **closed position**. Open position means the open strings are used and closed position means they are not used. To play both thirds in closed position, slide the left hand first finger up from the minor third to the major third (D - D#).

SIXTEENTH NOTE ROCK FEELS

This section covers several sixteenth note feels. Sixteenth notes receive a quarter of a beat in 4/4 time. To count sixteenth notes, use the syllables "e" and "a" for the notes between the beats and up beats (1 e & a 2 e & a 3 e & a 4 e & a). A good example of a sixteenth note feel is the bass line from the song "Goin' Down" by Jeff Beck, shown in Example 17.

CD 21 *Example 17*

In addition to the sixteenth-note feel, this example also uses a technique known as the **bend.** To bend the string, pull the fourth string down towards the third string until the pitch raises from A to B♭, then release the string to allow the pitch to return to A. It is helpful to use more than one finger in the left hand when bending a string, fretting the note with the third finger but keeping the first and second fingers on the string for support. Be sure to listen to make sure the bend is in tune.

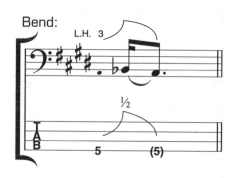

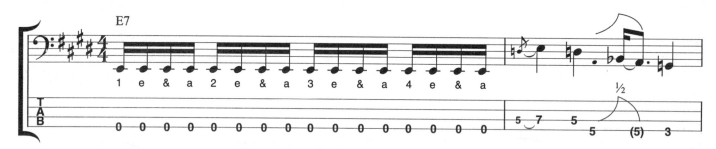

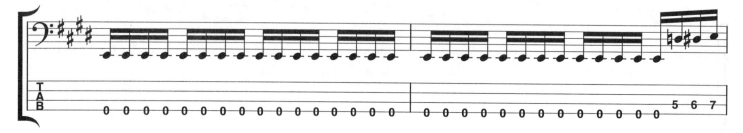

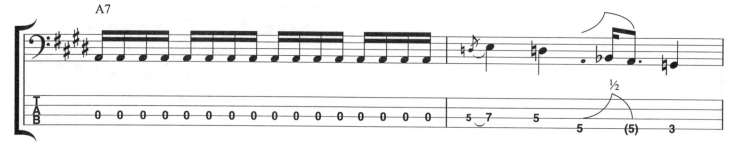

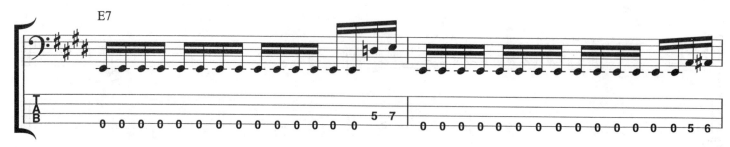

CD 22 *Example 18*

This example is similar to many of the bass lines played by Rocco Prestia from Tower of Power. The sixteenth notes move up chromatically to the root (E) and fifth (B) via connecting lines. Practice the example slowly at first to develop a clean attack, then slowly speed up. Use a metronome or drum machine.

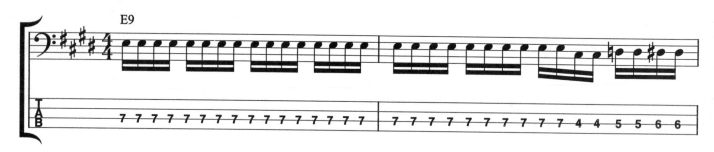

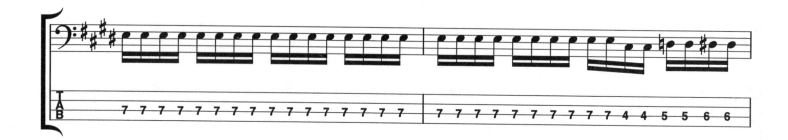

ROCK SHUFFLE AND BOOGIE FEELS

This next section deals primarily with rock shuffle feels. A shuffle is usually described as playing the eighth notes of a song with a triplet feel, where the eighth notes are played on the first and last part of the triplet. A triplet is playing three notes per beat and by cutting out the middle note, this gives you the shuffle feel. Shuffles are also written in 12/8 time, where there are 12 eighth notes per bar, grouped into four sets of three eighth notes. This is similar to playing four beats of triplets. Be sure to listen to the audio examples to hear the difference between the shuffle feels in this section and the "straight" feels in the previous sections.

CD ㉓ *Example 19*

Here is a simple shuffle feel, using mostly roots and simple chromatic lines approaching the chord changes. Remember to alternate the right hand fingers. This will help to play the shuffle feel at faster tempos.

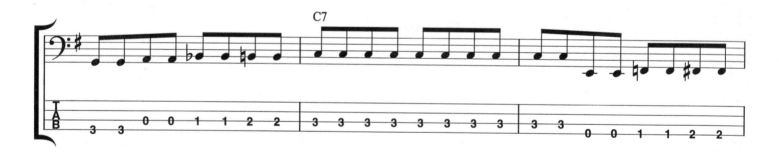

Example 20: Staccato Shuffle

Here is another shuffle that uses a staccato feel. Remember that to play staccato, simply lift the left hand finger off of the string for just a moment. You can see how the notes are cut off, which leaves just a tiny amount of space. That little bit of room between the notes makes the feel bounce just a little more than the legato feel.

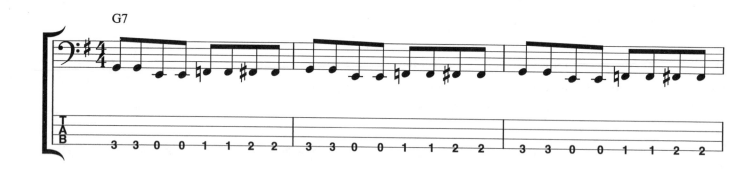

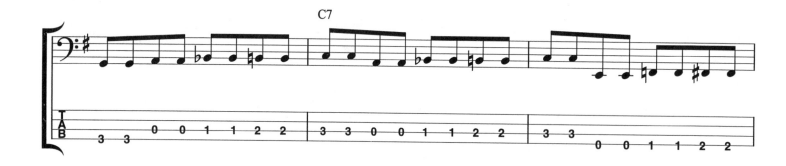

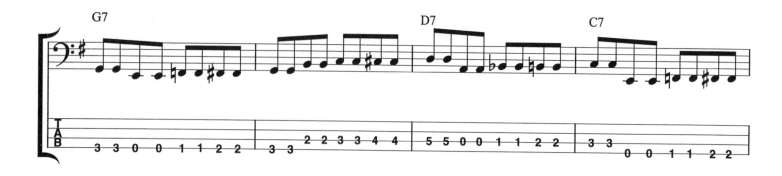

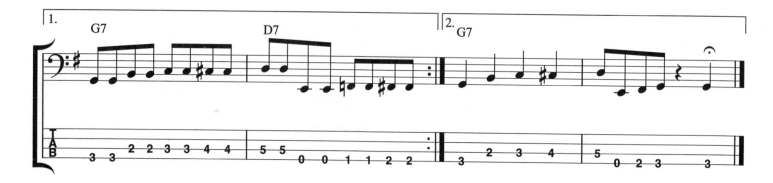

CD 25 *Example 21*

This example introduces another hammer-on technique, where the notes are sounded by hammering the string to the fretboard rather than the right hand attack. This example uses a triplet hammer-on in the left hand. The note is sounded by the right hand attack, then the second finger hammers on, followed by the third finger, in the rhythm of a triplet. Practice making the attack of the left hand sound similar to the attack of the right hand.

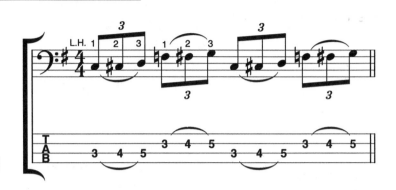

Example 22

This example is in the style known as the **Chicago shuffle**. The Chicago shuffle is characterized by its root down to the fifth movement, alternating shuffle eighth notes root–fifth (C–G). The example also uses connecting lines similar to those used in previous examples.

CD **27** *Example 23*

This example introduces the **boogie feel**. A boogie feel is a shuffle characterized by a constantly repeated bass figure, which is highly syncopated and stresses the up-beats over the down-beats. This feel is important to learn, due to the fact that rock music has been greatly influenced by boogie music. The important thing to remember about the boogie feel is that it is extremely syncopated, with most of the notes occurring on the up-beats.

Example 24

This example is similar to Example 22 only this time using **power chords**. A power chord is played by combining the root and the fifth together, and is similar to playing a major or minor triad without the third. This makes the power chord very popular in rock and blues because when improvising, both thirds can be used without clashing with the chords.

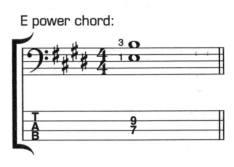

E power chord:

Example 25

This example is a boogie feel in 12/8, meaning there are 12 eighth notes per measure. This is similar to playing triplets in 4/4 time, much like a shuffle feel. The feel is set up by alternating the right hand fingers on the third and fourth strings. Remember to keep your right hand fingers in the same position and you will get a consistent sound.

12/8 feel:

Beats: 1 (2) 3 4 (5) 6 7 (8) 9 10 (11) 12

Triplet feel:

Beats: 1 (trip) let 2 (trip) let 3 (trip) let 4 (trip) let

CD
30 *Example 26*

This example is the primary riff from the tune "Lies" by Tim Bogart. Like Example 25, this example is in 12/8 and the triplet feel is set up by the right hand. The example alternates between the open fourth string root (E) and the 6 (C#), flat 7 (D) and octave on the third string, and ends with a very common descending minor pentatonic riff.

CD 31 *Example 27*

This example uses a major pentatonic pattern similar to Example 16, but this time uses shuffle eighth notes instead of straight eighth notes.

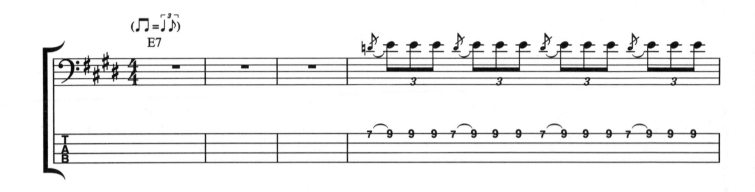

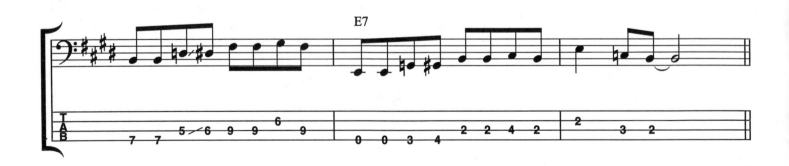

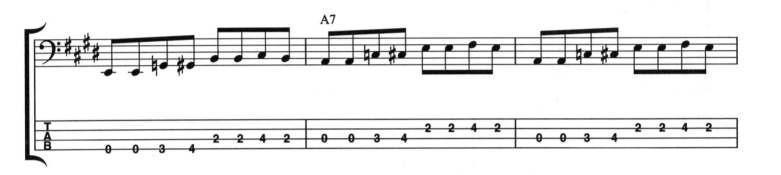

TAPPING, HARMONICS AND DOUBLE-STOPS

This section will cover some "tricky little bits" that work really well to impress people: tapping, harmonics and double-stops. **Tapping** is a fun thing, made popular by Billy Sheehan. While holding your left hand finger on the neck, you "tap" the note to the fretboard with the tip of your right hand index finger, then pull down on the string as you release the right hand note to sound the left hand note.

CD (32) Example 28

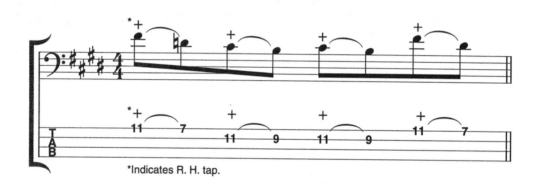

*Indicates R. H. tap.

Tapping can also be used in conjunction with left hand hammer-ons and pull-offs.

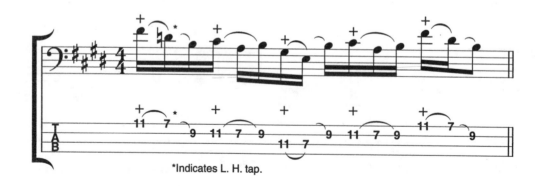

*Indicates L. H. tap.

CD
(33) *Example 29*

Harmonics are found at various points on the bass and can be used to play chords, melodies or just for effect. To play a harmonic on the bass, lightly touch the string directly over a fret (do not depress the string to the fretboard). Pluck with the picking hand. You should hear a ringing "bell" like sound.

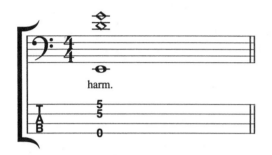

By combining more than one harmonic, they can be used to play chords. If you play the harmonics at the fifth fret on the first and second strings with the open fourth string, they combine to form a lovely E minor 7 chord.

Practice locating the various harmonics on the bass and experiment with using them in scales and chords.

CD
(34) *Example 30*

Double-stops are simply playing two notes at the same time. A common technique is to harmonize a scale using double-stops in a series of major and minor thirds, using the notes from that scale.

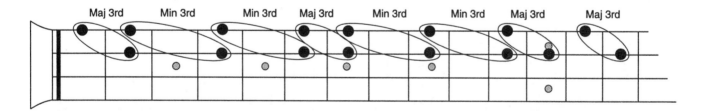

The example below shows the E mixolydian scale (which is the same as the A major scale starting on E) harmonized up to the octave, all played on the first two strings. After reaching the octave, the pattern repeats again (as far as the neck on your bass allows).

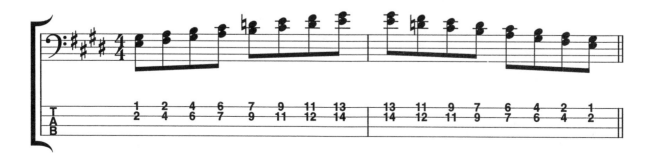

CD
(35) *Example 31*

This example combines two of the previous techniques into one exercise. It begins with the harmonics at the fifth and seventh frets, and then moves into the tapping section. Remember to start slowly and gradually increase the tempo using a metronome or drum machine.

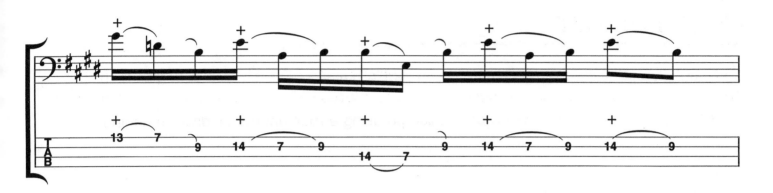

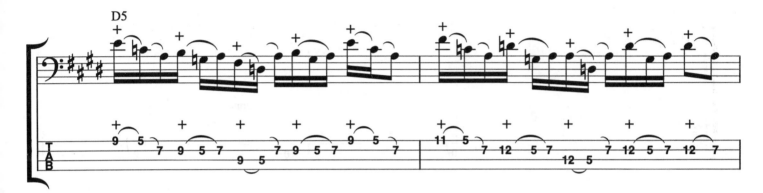

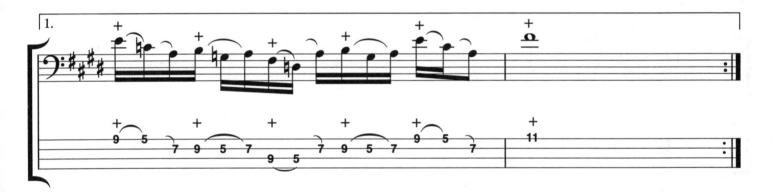

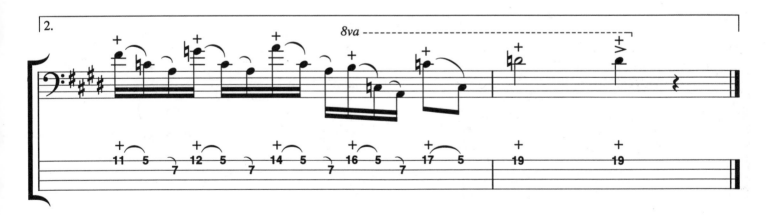

CD
36 *Example 32*

This exercise introduces a technique known as a "power slide," which is simply playing the fifth fret D power chord and sliding it up to the seventh fret E power chord. The example also uses the slash chord, where the third is used in the bass instead of the root.

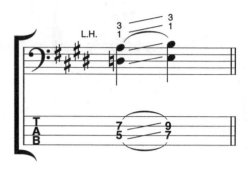

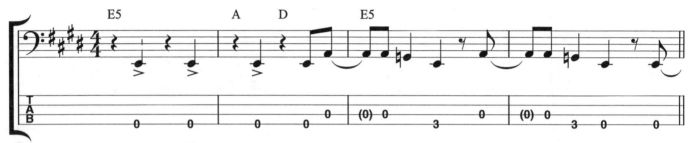

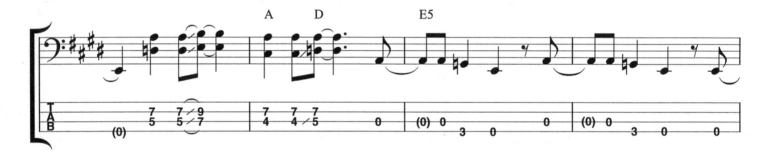

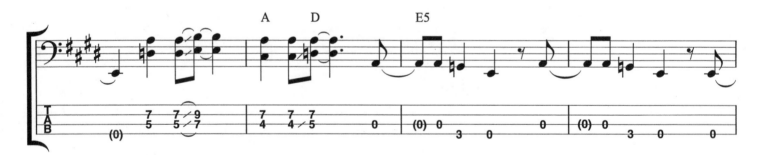

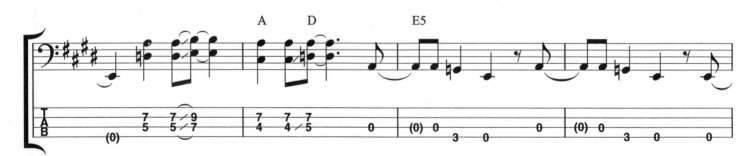

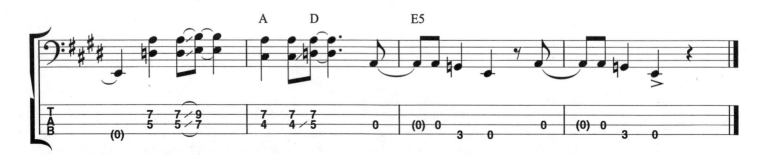